WILDLIFE
OF SERENGETI
& Ngorongoro Conservation Area

Jean du Plessis
Rupert Watson

Published by Struik Nature
(an imprint of Penguin Random House South
Africa (Pty) Ltd)
Reg. No. 1953/000441/07
The Estuaries No. 4, Oxbow Crescent, Century
Avenue, Century City, 7441
PO Box 1144, Cape Town, 8000, South Africa

Visit **www.struiknature.co.za** and join
the Struik Nature Club for updates, news,
events and special offers.

First published in 2025

10 9 8 7 6 5 4 3 2 1

Copyright © in text, 2025: Rupert Watson
Copyright © in photographs, 2025: Jean
du Plessis, and as indicated on page 190
Copyright © in maps, 2025: Penguin
Random House South Africa (Pty) Ltd,
Liezel Bohdanowicz
Copyright © in published edition, 2025:
Penguin Random House South Africa (Pty) Ltd

Publisher: Pippa Parker
Managing editor: Roelien Theron
Editor: Heléne Booyens
Designers: Heléne Booyens, Emily de Beer
Cartographer: Liezel Bohdanowicz
Proofreader: Thea Grobbelaar

MIX
Paper | Supporting
responsible forestry
FSC® C178225

Reproduction by Studio Repro
Printed and bound in China by
Golden Prosperity Industry Limited

All rights reserved. No part of this
publication may be reproduced,
stored in a retrieval system, or
transmitted, in any form or by any
means, electronic, mechanical,
photocopying, recording or otherwise,
without the prior written permission
of the copyright owner(s).

ISBN 978 1 77584 883 7 (Print)
ISBN 978 1 77584 884 4 (ePub)

Making illegal copies of this publication, distributing them unlawfully
or sharing them on social media without the written permission of
the publisher may lead to civil claims or criminal complaints.

Protect the communities who are sustained by creativity.

Contents

Introduction
4

Mammals
10

Birds
116

Reptiles
152

Frogs
166

Insects
168

Plants
176

Glossary / Picture credits / References / Index
189

INTRODUCTION

Established in 1951, the Serengeti National Park covers nearly 15,000km^2, preserving a great diversity of natural habitat. At over half that size, the adjacent Ngorongoro Conservation Area was declared a separate conservation area in 1959. The two combine to create one of the most spectacular wildlife destinations in the world. This book unveils the rich diversity of wildlife that this astonishing part of Africa supports, showcasing a large selection of mammals and birds, also reptiles, frogs and insects, as well as some of the plant life.

About the region

The principal environmental features of **Serengeti** are the grassy plains in the south, acacia savannah in the centre, wooded hills in the northern area, and quite extensive woodland along the river banks and in the west. A variety of plains, rivers, lakes, hills and rocky outcrops are found throughout, each of which has its own particular character.

In **Ngorongoro** is a magnificent crater with the famous Lake Magadi at the bottom (*magadi* is the Swahili word for 'soda'), renowned for its spectacular flocks of lesser flamingos and herds of grazing game.

Combined, Serengeti and Ngorongoro are home to a vast array of wildlife, including the Big Five – lion, leopard, elephant, buffalo and rhino – as well as cheetah, giraffe, hippo and a multitude of different antelope species. Each year, thousands of visitors from all corners of the world come here to view the annual migration of over 1.5 million wildebeest and half a million zebra. These animals travel to fresh grazing grounds alongside gazelles and eland, with a slew of predators following. Besides these large mammals, a mass of smaller animals also call this wonderland home.

Right, from the top: Cheetah siblings, impala, lesser flamingos, fruiting sausage tree.
Opposite: White-bearded wildebeest cross the Mara River.

Viewing notes

Different habitats host different wildlife. To make the most of your visit, be sure to visit varying areas of the park.

WATERBODIES There are going to be more birds and animals wherever there is water. Many animals have to drink every day, and a lot of birds are specifically adapted to live in or around marshes, lakes and rivers. Some of the lakes are alkaline, such as Lake Mastek (near Lake Ndutu), Lake Magadi (further north in Serengeti) and of course the lake of the same name in Ngorongoro Crater. These alkaline lakes attract very different birds than fresher waters do, and are less palatable for animals to drink.

GRASSY PLAINS Wildebeest, zebra and other large quadrupeds congregate on the grassy plains in the south of the park during the rainy season. As the short grass begins to wither, they move to areas with longer grass, which are home to ostriches, topi and mixed herds of gazelles. Perhaps a secretarybird will put in an appearance, stalking through the herbage in search of a snake.

SERONERA The central area of Seronera is known as the Big Cat Capital for good reason. Leopards can be found resting languidly on the branches of acacia or sausage trees. As the day heats up, prides of lion retreat into the shadows. Earlier, they might be found warming

up on the rocky kopjes, which are always worth searching out, whether for lions, hyraxes, klipspringers, mongooses or any one of a variety of special birds.

WOODLAND North of Seronera, towards Kenya's Maasai Mara National Reserve, the tree cover is thicker. There may be more giraffes up here and perhaps the chance of seeing an elephant. The riverine forest down the edges of the Mara River hosts many birds unlikely to be seen elsewhere. In the deeper pools, hippo pods rest up in the day, particularly visible when water levels are low. Then, too, crocodiles may be easier to find, warming up on mud banks.

WESTERN CORRIDOR Turning left at Seronera, the Western Corridor road follows close to the Grumeti River, where not only hippos and crocodiles are sure to show themselves, but also, at the right time of year, thousands of migrating wildebeest. At the end of the Corridor is the Ndabaka Gate and from there it is only a few kilometres to the shores of Lake Victoria.

The area's original inhabitants, the Maasai, live all around the edges of Serengeti and within the Ngorongoro Conservation Area.

Ngorongoro – a unique heritage

The Ngorongoro Conservation Area was declared a UNESCO World Heritage Site in 1979, in recognition of its importance as a site for biodiversity and conservation. In 2010, it was also inscribed as a cultural site because of its rich fossil record, which traces human evolution, and the interaction between humans and the environment spanning almost four million years. Although a wildlife sanctuary, Ngorongoro is managed as a multi-use area, balancing the needs of wildlife and those of the indigenous Maasai and their livestock, although the Maasai are increasingly less pastoral.

Large mammals are the main attraction in Serengeti and Ngorongoro, but they are only part of the region's intricate web of life, woven over millions of years. These granite plugs were once surrounded by softer bedrock, eroded away by wind and water, leaving a perfect lookout kopje for this lion.

WHITE-BEARDED WILDEBEEST The wildebeest migration is a legendary event, taking hundreds of thousands of these animals, and their calves, from the short-grass plains of Ngorongoro and the southern Serengeti on a huge, almost year-long loop. The herds begin their northward move in May or June, reaching the Maasai Mara in Kenya two or three months later. On the way they will have to ford the Grumeti River, and then the Mara River, where this picture was taken.

MATING SEASON Wildebeest calves are born within a month of each other, usually at the beginning of the year. When the rains begin to ease off, in May and June, and animals start their migration, a short period of frenzied mating takes place as mature males try to breed with as many females as possible. This brief mating season, known as the rut, sees more experienced males try and defend their temporary territories against incursions from younger ones.

In May, the rainy season is ending and the wildebeest gather on the short-grass plains, ready to begin their annual migration.

MIGRATION HERDS Wildebeest are often accompanied on their migration by large numbers of plains zebra, as well as herds of Thomson's gazelle and other antelope. The zebra travel in smaller groups within the huge herds of wildebeest, sometimes leading and grazing down the long grass in advance of their travelling companions, who prefer it shorter.

Wildebeest, also known as gnus, belong to the Bovidae family. The females are slightly smaller than the males and both sexes have horns.

CALVES Potential predators always lie in wait, whether in water or on dry land, especially for newly born zebra and wildebeest calves. These risk being trampled in the chaos of water crossings, where crocodiles lurk, or falling prey on the open plains to lion, cheetahs and spotted hyaenas, which are always trailing the herds of herbivores on the lookout for stragglers. Newborn wildebeest calves are up on their feet within 10 minutes of birth, but move more slowly than the rest of the herd for some days, when they are particularly vulnerable. Once absorbed into the herd, calves remain with their mothers until these produce the next crop of young. The animals' average lifespan is around 20 years, but they have been known to reach twice that age.

Cheetahs detect prey by sight and so make for the high points in otherwise flat terrain. This one has found an old termite mound from which to survey its territory.

ZEBRA 'Are we white with black stripes, or black with white stripes?' asks the cartoon zebra foal. Well, if you look closely, you'll see that there is more white fur on a zebra (particularly on its belly) than there is black. But, if you were to shave off a zebra's fur, you would be left with black skin.

Like giraffes, each zebra's pattern is different, enabling individuals to be recognised, like bar codes. What is the benefit of these stripes? The list of possible advantages is long and headed by: cryptic camouflage in poor light, confusing pursuing predators, and thermoregulation.

Zebra are grazers, and live mostly in family groups of a single stallion and several mares and their offspring. When migrating alongside the wildebeest, many of these groups may travel together

in a larger herd. As so often with savannah wildlife, surplus males gather into bachelor groups, lurking around the edges of the herds. There, it is usually the task of the mother to protect her young, but if obvious danger threatens, foals will be urged into the middle of a protective ring of adults.

The Ngorongoro Crater is a caldera – the collapsed remnants of a once-active volcano. The intact rim all around effectively creates its own ecosystem, which is home to nearly all of East Africa's large quadrupeds. As the clouds start to lift, Lake Magadi appears in the distance.

ELEPHANT There are two similar species in Africa, the bush or savannah elephant, which is the one occurring throughout most of East Africa, and the forest elephant. Elephants are easily the biggest terrestrial mammals in the world, weighing up to 6,000kg.

Have a good look at the ears of this remarkable mammal. You might expect the external opening of the ear to be behind the flaps, as with dogs for instance, but rather they are in front of the flaps. The flaps' huge surface area funnels sounds into the ears. Flapping the ears also helps cool the elephant down.

Herds comprise related females of all ages, as well as some young males before these leave to join bachelor groups.

HERD LIFE Elephants live in herds, guided everywhere they go by an older female, the matriarch, whose store of knowledge helps the herd to find food and water. She makes the decisions on what to eat, where to go next, and also slows the herd down when there are newborn calves around.

Cows may produce their first calf when around 12 years old, after a gestation period of 22 months – the longest of any mammal. They give birth standing up. The mother will suckle her calf for four years, by which time she may be preparing to give birth again, adding a new calf to the herd every four or five years. Youngsters are cared for by the whole herd of related females, which creates a society of mutual protection.

Like all social mammals, elephants have a highly sophisticated system of communication, including detecting vibrations through the soles of their feet. Recent research suggests that elephants can recognise the distinct calls of separate individuals from far away.

MAMMALS

BULLS Young bulls usually leave their natal herd to join bachelor groups of single males when they are around 15 years old. There they joust among themselves for perhaps the next 10 years, loosely establishing a pecking order. By the time they are 25, bulls start showing signs of coming into musth. This is an annual occurrence, typically lasting two or three months, and may continue until the elephant is 55 or 60. A bull in musth secretes temporin from the temporal gland between the eye and ear. These pungent secretions are easily visible running down the elephant's cheeks. They are a sign of increased testosterone, driving aggressive behaviour and an enhanced interest in the opposite sex. This might lead to them joining family herds and testing to see which females are receptive to their advances.

TUSKS AND TRUNKS The ivory tusks are enlarged incisor teeth, first starting to show on both males and females when the animals are around three years old, then growing continuously for the rest of their lives. Tusks measuring as long as 3.5m along the outer curve and weighing more than 100kg have been recorded.

Elephants have nostrils at the end of their trunk, through which they breathe, smell and trumpet. The trunk is also used to draw up water to squirt into the mouth or over the body as well as being an essential in grooming themselves or touching and stroking others.

CALVES One of the consequences of spending 22 months in their mother's womb is that calves are born very mature; they are able to stand within an hour of birth and to walk fast enough to keep up with the herd within a couple of days, so it can carry on moving in search of food or water.

For the first year of their life, calves are small enough to pass underneath the adults' bellies. For four years, the mother will continue to suckle the young one from mammary glands between her front legs.

FEEDING A very inefficient digestive system requires elephants to eat up to 150kg of food a day – grass, leaves and shrubs, depending on what's around. Much of the meal exits undigested in their dung. Elephants are also partial to any bark that is rich in water, minerals and roughage.

In theory, elephants continue growing all their lives, which might be 60 or 70 years. Then they often die of starvation because their back molar teeth are so worn down that they are no longer able to chew food.

MUD BATHING Elephants have very thick skin, its creases and wrinkles helping with water retention. As such, a soak in the mud keeps an elephant cool for a good while. They need to drink and bathe at least every three days, and in times of drought may resort to digging holes in dry river beds using their feet, tusks and trunks.

MAMMALS

BLACK RHINOCEROS This huge animal, the biggest in Africa after the elephant, is more easily seen in Ngorongoro Crater than in Serengeti. The other African rhino, the white rhino, is not found in either. Both species are now in desperate need of protection, having been victims of terrible persecution, first by settlers and hunters, and then by poachers as the demand for their horns rocketed. These are still sought after in the Far East, either for additives to traditional medicine or as status symbols.

Black rhinos are solitary animals, except for mothers and calves, who remain together until the young are between two and four years old. They are browsers, not grazers, and so are best searched for in bushland, rather than on open grass plains. They use their pointed upper lips to help pluck leaves and branches from a wide variety of vegetation. Rhinos have very poor eyesight, relying more on hearing and smell to detect potential dangers.

Not for nothing is the name hippopotamus a combination of two Greek words, *hippo* for 'horse' and *potamos* for 'river'. These river horses spend all day in the mud or the water, before leaving at night to feed on grass and occasional fruits, sometimes travelling as far as 5km from their aquatic home.

MAMMALS

HIPPOPOTAMUS The hippo's eyes, ears and nose are all on top of its head, meaning that they protrude from the water while the rest of the body is almost completely submerged.

The jaws are hinged in such a way as to be able almost to open 180 degrees. Big incisor and canine teeth grow out of the lower jaw, but these are of more use in fighting than eating. When out at night feeding, hippos use their lips to nibble off the grass, then chew it before swallowing.

Hippo skin may be as much as 6cm thick and is dark in colour overall, apart from paler, pinky patches around the cheeks and eyes and on the belly. The skin secretes a natural sunblock, which allows the animals to stay out of the water for an hour or two without their skin cracking or burning. However, in extreme conditions, hippos do their best to immerse themselves in whatever mud remains for as long as they can before moving off in search of other water.

When river levels fall, hippos can be squeezed into fewer and fewer shrinking pools, so that in the end there may not be room to fully submerge themselves. Then birds can easily walk over their backs (here a common moorhen), and oxpeckers, in particular, search out ticks and other insects in the animals' skin. Sometimes cattle egrets perch on their host's back. Birds can also serve as an early warning system, alerting the animals to approaching danger by the very action of flying away.

These are Masai giraffes, one of several distinct giraffe subspecies and the national animal of Tanzania. The Swahili word for giraffe is *twiga*.

GIRAFFE The collective noun for giraffes on the move is a journey or a tower. Surprisingly perhaps, the neck of a giraffe has not elongated by the addition of more vertebrae, but rather through the elongation of their seven vertebrae, which is the same number as in the human neck. Having such long necks requires all sorts of physiological adaptations, not least a complex valve system to ensure that blood reaches the head when the animal is upright, but that the pressure is not too great when the head is down, drinking. To drink, the giraffe has to splay out its legs and maybe also bend them, making it awkwardly vulnerable.

It is not unusual to find several young giraffes together, with one of the mothers keeping a not-very-watchful eye over the crèche. It is debatable as to how well this system works, as there is a high rate of predation on the young, and some researchers reckon that only a quarter of the young make it to maturity.

Giraffes are ruminants, with four stomachs, and much of the day and a lot of the night is spent chewing the cud.

Both sexes have two bony protrusions from their head, and as they age males develop bumps on their skulls which can resemble a third horn. Males indulge in 'necking' combat, using their necks as weapons to win the right to mate with particular females.

Like zebra, each individual giraffe has its own distinctive coat pattern.

WARTHOG These hogs with protective calluses on their faces – the 'warts' – are never far from water and are otherwise common throughout the savannah and in lightly wooded country. When sensing danger, groups run off in a line, adults with their narrow tails raised vertically, until they reach their burrows. There they often turn about and reverse down into safety, preferring to face any danger head on. They are quite able to dig their own burrows, but prefer to take over those abandoned by aardvarks or other animals.

Both sexes sport two pairs of tusks protruding upwards from the mouth. The upper ones are particularly prominent, and are used not for digging, but rather for defence or attack.

One of the warthog's most peculiar habits is that of feeding on its knees. A combination of short neck and long legs seems to encourage this.

MAMMALS

AFRICAN BUFFALO Both males and females have heavy curling horns, but those of the male are joined at the forehead, creating a boss, which is one way to ascertain a buffalo's sex.

Perhaps surprisingly for such large creatures, they are ruminants, and after a prolonged spell of grazing grass, they spend much of the day chewing the cud. In times of drought, buffalo may be the first of the savannah animals to lose condition and, if dry times continue, to die. They are heavily dependent on water, needing to drink every day and, at times, to wallow in mud, both for thermoregulation and to rid themselves of biting insects.

African buffalo may congregate in huge herds of several hundred animals, especially during the rainy season, at the end of which calves start to arrive. The gestation period is some 340 days. Females have their first calves when four or five years of age. Their average lifespan is about 12 years.

The fused horn base is known as a boss.

A single lion is no match for a mature bull.

HERD LIFE Living in herds is a defensive mechanism to prevent individuals, whether mature or young, being singled out by predators, particularly lions. If these are after buffalo, they will usually need to hunt in a group to bring down a mature one. Dominant males may join the herds temporarily to mate, otherwise these are comprised predominantly of females and young. Surplus males spend most of their time in bachelor groups, sometimes made up of young bulls and sometimes older ones. Really old bulls are often edged out to live on their own, and should be avoided at all costs. Buffalo in herds are far less aggressive and tend to move off together. The animals have a poor sense of hearing and sight and mostly rely on smell.

When a herd of buffalo is in among long grass, its presence might first be revealed by a flying flock of cattle egrets, which are mainly after the insects disturbed by the animals' progress through the grass.

LION Not for nothing is this predator called the 'Lion King'. These overlords of the animal kingdom are indeed the ultimate symbol of strength and bravery, and are right at the top of the food chain.

There used to be lions in northern Africa, but these have gone, and now they are found only south of the Sahara. In those parts of Africa where they still occur, lions occupy most habitats other than desert and dense forest, much obviously depending on the availability of prey and absence of human disturbance.

LIVING IN PRIDES Lions are unusual so far as cats go in that they are social animals, living together in prides. These generally comprise several related females, their cubs, and one or more unrelated males. Lionesses may remain in their home pride all their lives, but males are forced out when two or three years old. They then roam around until they are ready to challenge other males with established prides and force them out. Often no longer able to hunt for themselves, old lions may eventually starve to death. The new males are now responsible for defending their pride's territory, marking its bounds with squirts of urine and roaring aggressively as the light fails. Roars ease off to grunts later in the night.

HUNTING Lions hunt mostly at night or at dawn, preying particularly on wildebeest, antelope and buffalo, especially when the latter are weakened in droughts. In the dark, they first stalk their prey, preferring to get some 20m away before charging. Lions can reach speeds of 60km/h, but only for short distances. They seldom attempt longer pursuits.

Most of the hunting is done by groups of females, some taking on the role of chasers, others killers, biting the throat of their prey to strangle it. However, these hunting females may still have to defer to the males when it comes to enjoying the fruits of their efforts, with adult males first in line to eat at a kill.

RESTING UP Lions usually eat once every two or three days, gorging themselves when they do, so much of their rest time is spent digesting their last meal. They spend perhaps three-quarters of the day resting, usually in the shade of bushes or leafy trees, which is where to look for them when it is hot. They are also partial to lazing in trees, not least to escape bothersome clouds of flies.

BREEDING Mating can take place at any time of the year, although it is best for both parties if they are well fed and so have no need to satisfy hunger pangs as well as sexual desire! Bouts of mating may last for up to a week, and on particularly energetic days the couple can mate twice or three times an hour, or over 50 times a day. Coitus seldom lasts more than a minute, often less.

LION CUBS Gestation lasts around 15 weeks, at the end of which a litter of two to six cubs is born. These are born blind and only start to open their eyes after a week or so. During the early weeks, the cubs are very vulnerable and their mother goes to great lengths to hide them in rocky outcrops or particularly thick cover. The survival rate among lion cubs is surprisingly low. The young often have difficulty in finding space to feed on a kill,

although male lions may allow their own cubs in. Along with starvation, infanticide is a common cause of death, particularly when a new male takes over a pride and kills the unrelated cubs, so ensuring the future success of his own genes. Young cubs have faint spots all over their bodies, which disappear as they mature. They are raised jointly by the pride's females and will suckle from any lioness with milk.

CHEETAH The animal's name comes from the Hindi word *chita*, meaning 'spotted' or 'variegated'. These spots are round, unlike the leopard's, and black tear marks run down the side of the cheetah's small face, which may help to reduce the sunlight glare. These cats are usually solitary, but some males live in coalitions, often of siblings, which play with and groom each other.

Resting on top of one of the Gol Kopjes enables this cat to get some peace, as well as giving it an unparalleled view over the grassland where prey may be grazing.

HUNTING Cheetahs tend to stalk their prey until this is no more than 50m away, and then make their celebrated sprints in pursuit, reaching top speeds of 120km/h. They are the fastest land animals in the world, but sprint for very short distances, maybe 200 or 300m. The cheetah is the only cat that cannot fully retract its claws, giving it added grip on the ground.

Hunting by sight, in relatively open country, cheetahs are inevitably diurnal. The preferred prey in Serengeti is Thomson's gazelle, although when the wildebeest are calving, young are prime targets, however well parentally protected they may seem.

Males living in coalitions will most likely hunt cooperatively.

Once upon its prey, a cheetah tends to trip the animal and knock it over before suffocating it with a bite to the throat. When the hunter has stopped panting from all that concentrated exertion, it will try and eat as quickly as possible, because it is easily deterred from its kill by approaching lions, hyaenas or jackals. If possible, the prey is dragged into some sort of cover.

Top and above: This cheetah had killed a wildebeest calf, but the mother continued to guard her dead young one. The cheetah is not strong enough to face up to an aggresive, mature wildebeest.

CHEETAH CUBS Mothers may have anything up to eight cubs, but they more often have three or four. These newborns are extremely vulnerable, arriving with their eyes closed, and unable to walk for at least 10 days. The female keeps the young in a den, which she changes every few days. Later, in the course of teaching her young ones to hunt, she may bring back live young gazelles for the cubs to learn to chase and catch.

LEOPARD These spotted cats are much bulkier than cheetahs, largely nocturnal and very agile climbers of trees, which they are also able to descend head first. A mature leopard can drag a prey animal much heavier than its own weight up a tree, preventing scavenging lions or hyaenas from stealing its kill on the ground. In general, however, leopards prefer catching prey smaller and lighter than themselves.

They have a preference for rocky habitat, particularly mothers who are anxious to hide away their cubs while they go off patrolling their territory or hunting. The gestation period is around 100 days, after which two, sometimes three cubs are born.

The mother keeps her young hidden for up to eight weeks, moving them from one den to another. During most of this time the cubs are suckling, until the mother brings some meat. For the next two years, the cubs remain with their mother as she gradually teaches them all the tricks of self-sufficiency.

Females take cubs on their first hunting expeditions at around four months, but it

will be some time before they are old enough to hunt for themselves and a lot longer before they get to chase the preferred prey of adult leopards – like wildebeest, impala and olive baboons. The latter have distinctive danger calls for different predators, and en masse can also pose a real threat to hunting leopards.

While females seem more diurnal in their hunting habits, males are particularly active at night. The animals' rasping night-time calls are often likened to someone sawing wood.

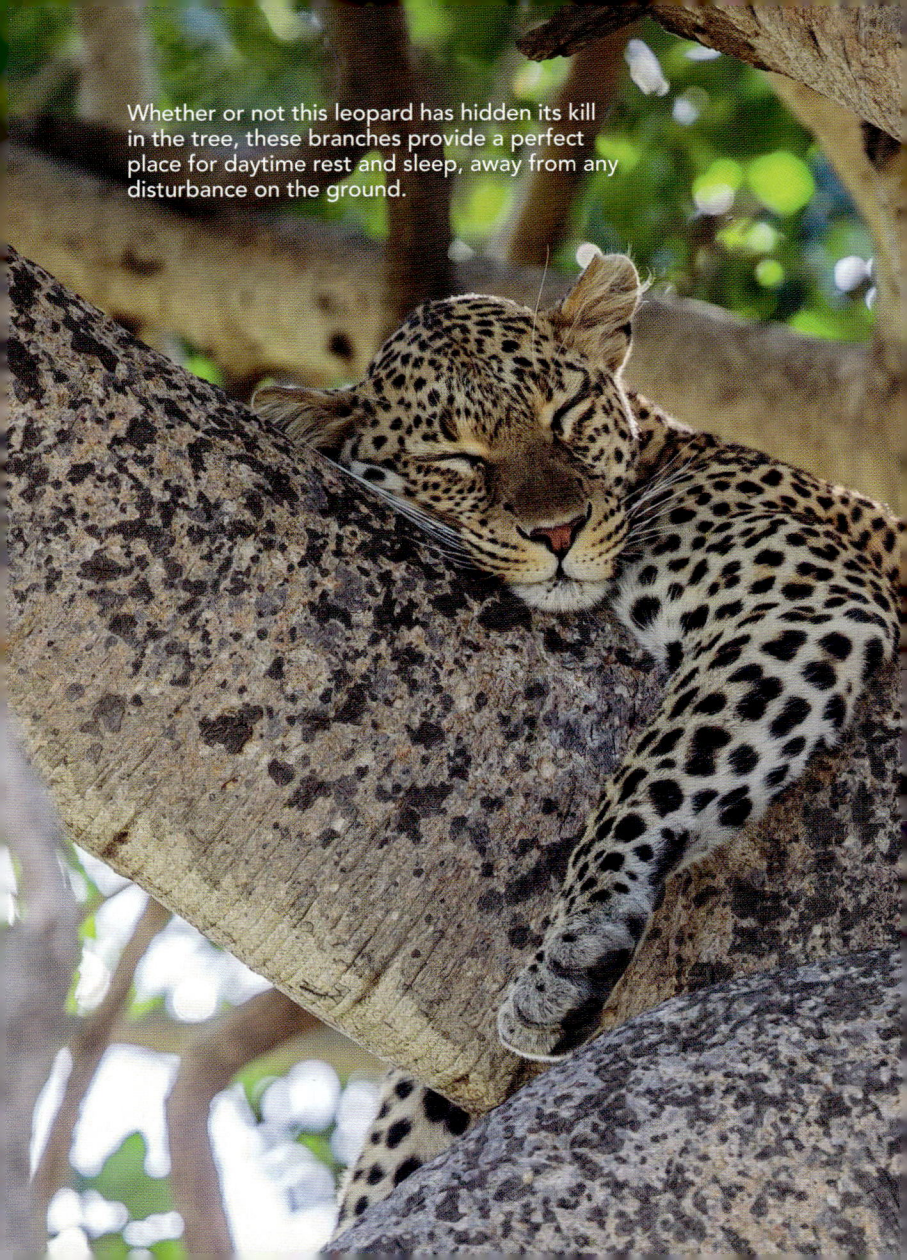

Whether or not this leopard has hidden its kill in the tree, these branches provide a perfect place for daytime rest and sleep, away from any disturbance on the ground.

Caracal

Serval

CARACAL Instantly recognisable by its long black ear tufts and usually chestnut-coloured coat, the caracal is an elusive cat, not least because it is largely nocturnal. It is mainly carnivorous, hunting small mammals and birds. Being a great jumper, a caracal sometimes snatches birds from the air.

SERVAL A small, long-legged spotted cat, the serval is a solitary carnivore that might even attack small antelope. It can also jump high in the air, and large ears enable it to locate smaller prey in thick grass. This it stalks until it is close enough to pounce, killing the victim with a bite to the neck.

AFRICAN WILD CAT This species is distributed all over Africa, looking very like the closely related domestic cats, with which it freely interbreeds. It is not easy to find anywhere, being a stealthy hunter of all kinds of small animal prey and usually active in early morning or late evening.

African wild cat

SPOTTED HYAENA There is a guilty look about a single hyaena, slinking back in the early morning to its den, likely having purloined this shelter from a warthog or aardvark. Despite appearances, it is a member of a highly successful species, made particularly so by its being both scavenger and hunter. It will happily dive into carcasses of animals other carnivores have killed, or otherwise hunt down its own prey, usually in groups, by chasing it until the animal collapses from exhaustion. In Serengeti, the preferred prey animals are wildebeest, zebra and Thomson's gazelle, not least because these animals are the most abundant.

Females are larger than males. Social life revolves around communities known as clans, which occupy communal dens, often with many different entrances. Hyaenas communicate either through repetitive *whoo-oops* or their famous laugh.

The spotted hyaena's extensive range overlaps with that of brown and striped hyaenas, but the spotted inevitably dominates.

Both the black-backed jackal and the hyaena seem quite oblivious of the other's presence.

STRIPED HYAENA Larger than the aardwolf but smaller than the spotted hyaena, this is another nocturnal creature that is not likely to be seen in the daytime. A long, hairy crest runs down the whole of its back. It subsists more on bones and older mammalian carrion than do other hyaenas. In areas where spotted hyaenas are also found, the striped is much more retiring and less territorial.

As well as the striped and spotted hyaenas, there is a brown hyaena, but this lives only in southern Africa. These, together with the aardwolf, comprise the Hyaenidae family.

AARDWOLF This shy animal is rarely encountered owing to its nocturnal habits, resting up in dens during the day. It is in the hyaena family, and with stripes and a long, hairy mane down its neck and back, it does indeed bear a superficial resemblance to the striped hyaena. However, it is neither a scavenger nor a predator of mammals; fascinatingly, it is insectivorous, surviving almost exclusively on harvester termites. It locates underground colonies by sound and smell, then licks up thousands of termites using its long, broad, sticky tongue. In very wet weather, aardwolves may look for other insects or forage for eggs.

BAT-EARED FOX A group of these endearing foxes usually comprises an adult pair and their young. If they look to be living a life of easy relaxation when you see them outside their burrow, it is because they do most of their hunting at night!

They are carnivores, but largely insectivorous, and their preferred food is harvester termites. If these are not available, then beetles and other invertebrates will do. They have much smaller teeth than any other foxes, and more of them (often as many as 50) that are adapted to crushing insects. Huge ears enable them to detect termite activity well below the earth's surface, and, having heard it, they then scrabble away with their strong front paws until they reach the insects.

Black-backed jackal

Side-striped jackal

Black-backed jackals

BLACK-BACKED JACKAL These innocent-looking canids are those most likely to be seen on game drives, especially in the morning. They are more diurnal than the side-striped and golden jackals, and, while usually solitary, black-backed jackals sometimes also hunt in family groups. When pursuing prey cooperatively, they may try to bring down a small antelope or newborn wildebeest, but otherwise, invertebrates, carrion and even fallen fruits are all grist to their digestive mills. The carrion may include pickings from kills made by larger carnivores.

Jackals are known to pair for life. Litters of three to six pups are first suckled and then fed on regurgitated food. At around six months of age, the youngsters will be hunting for themselves.

SIDE-STRIPED JACKAL This jackal is silvery and pale, rather than brown in colour, with a diagonal, whitish stripe down its flanks and a white tip to the tail. It is slightly smaller than other jackal species, which makes it less inclined to hunt its own mammalian prey. Side-striped jackals are monogamous, and their distribution is, to some extent, governed by the availability of dens.

The white-backed vulture and the jackal are probably both vying for the same remnants of a carcass.

GOLDEN JACKAL Also called the common jackal, this species is more used to drier country than the other jackals and, unlike these others, its range extends outside Africa. Omnivorous, golden jackals sometimes take nourishment from carrion where they may find themselves competing with other scavengers. Sandy colouring and a black tip to the tail are usually enough to confirm identification.

HONEY BADGER Also known as ratels, these short, stocky animals are silvery grey above, from forehead to tail, and black underneath. They are generally solitary and are omnivorous. Their front paws are armed with ferocious claws with which they dig for insects and other underground prey, and to facilitate this, they have internal ears which can be closed to keep out the earth as they dig. Honey badgers are also particularly aggressive when threatened, even towards humans. The 'honey' in their names derives from their particular fondness for attacking bees' nests, as much for the bee pupae and larvae as for the honey itself. They are often led to these nests by the greater honeyguide, a bird appropriately named by science as *Indicator indicator*!

MAMMALS

SMALL-SPOTTED GENET Genets are cat-like creatures with distinctly ringed tails at least as long as their bodies. The small-spotted genet is also known as the common genet, largely because it is widely distributed throughout Africa, and is not easily distinguished from the large-spotted genet, also found in East Africa. Both species may indulge their opportunistic, omnivorous tastes at feeding stations around lodges and camps. Adults are solitary except during the mating season or when a female is accompanied by her young, which were most likely born in a tree hollow.

All genets are renowned for their pungent scent glands, which they rub vigorously against twigs and branches, leaving signals as to their fertility.

CIVET Civets and genets are both in the Viverridae family, those in Africa distinguished by the former being largely terrestrial and the latter arboreal. As civets are nocturnal, or at best, crepuscular, these stripey-spotted, cat-like carnivores (although actually related to mongooses) are difficult to see, even though they live almost exclusively on the ground. They may stick to well-established paths in their hunt for small rodent prey, so if guides are aware of such paths, there is a better chance of finding these uncommon animals.

Dwarf mongoose

MONGOOSE These small, terrestrial carnivores in the Herpestidae family all feed on insects, worms, lizards, birds and their eggs. Some species are solitary, such as the slender mongoose, but others, including the banded and dwarf mongooses, are social creatures. Banded mongooses in particular are cooperative hunters, and there can be no more alarming prospect for a sitting mother bird than sensing their approach. Banded mongooses will also attack venomous snakes, being partially immune to their bites.

Slender mongoose

Banded mongoose

Steenbok

Nyala

Eland

Klipspringer

Naivasha dik-dik

Coke's hartebeest

ANTELOPE In Serengeti and Ngorongoro, antelope are a diverse group, ranging from petite duikers, dik-diks and klipspringers to much larger topi, eland and waterbuck. All gazelles are antelope too, as are impala. Unlike deer, which shed their antlers every year, those of antelope keep growing all their lives. Interestingly, some females, like those of Thomson's and Grant's gazelles, have horns, albeit smaller ones, while females of the closely related impala do not. Never is this more apparent than when a lyre-horned male impala is rounding up his harem of females!

Oribi

Thomson's gazelle

Grant's gazelle

Defassa waterbuck

Impala

Bohor reedbuck

Topi

Grey duiker

Thomson's gazelles are essentially social animals, as here, where the herd is grazing peacefully on the floor of Ngorongoro Crater.

THOMSON'S GAZELLE Named after the explorer Joseph Thomson and often referred to as 'Tommies', these antelope are distinguished from Grant's gazelle by the brown on their backs stretching all the way down to the tail, and by a distinctive black stripe down their flanks. Females have horns too, which they use to defend their calves, but nothing like the size of those of the males. These gazelles are particularly abundant on the short-grass plains of Serengeti. There they undergo minor migrations, during which they are often preyed upon by cheetahs. Gazelles are fast runners, zigzagging as they go, and pursuing predators are often confused by the number of animals in the herd, scattering in all directions.

GRANT'S GAZELLE Another species named after a European explorer, this time James Grant, these gazelles have distinctive white rumps that extend above their tails over onto their backs. They are larger than Thomson's gazelles, with which they frequently mix, and often graze in similar short-grass habitat. However, Grant's are also browsers, and far better adapted to drier conditions, when they can go for long without drinking water. Both species can also be found in Ngorongoro Crater, tending to keep out of long grass where predators may hide. Females give birth away from the herd, hiding the calf for at least a month before bringing it back to join the others. Subspecies are distinguished by different shaped horns.

ELAND This is the largest of all African antelope. Cattle-sized, it takes its name from the Dutch word for 'moose'. Eland are notoriously skittish, and gregarious, and it is hard to get close to a herd. In the photograph below, they are trotting away, followed by a large flock of wattled starlings, which often behave in the same way as oxpeckers, searching animal skin for ticks. Males and females sport twisted horns, and both also have fleshy dewlaps hanging below their necks. With age, the male's dewlap continues to extend down until almost reaching knee level, while the mane and forehead get bushier and darker. Despite their size, eland are prodigious jumpers and are estimated to be able to clear a 3m fence from a standing start. They browse more than they graze, so look for them in scrub rather than on the open plains.

COKE'S HARTEBEEST The Swahili name for this antelope is *kongoni*. It has a long, narrow face, made all the more so by horns, on both sexes, which look to have been added onto the skull as an afterthought! The hartebeest is generally the same shape as its close relative, the topi, but prefers to graze in longer grass. They live in herds, and females calve every 10 months or so. For a fortnight the calf is hidden away, and thereafter follows its mother well beyond the time she has her next offspring.

KLIPSPRINGER This tiny animal is found only in rocky areas, which it traverses almost as if on tiptoe. Only the males have short, thin horns. Klipspringers browse on young plants, including succulents, and are usually able to get enough water from their food without resorting to drinking.

OLIVE BABOON Baboons live in harems comprising a dominant male, maybe younger males, and then females and young. Males are easily recognisable as such, being larger, with longer muzzles and long-haired manes. Baboons are largely terrestrial and troops are most likely to be seen foraging on the ground for a wide variety of food, their cosmopolitan diet being one of the main reasons for their success as a species. It is well worth spending time watching baboon interactions, even in troops hanging out near human habitation. Mothers carry babies either on their backs, or clinging to their bellies, and one baboon always seems ready to groom another.

Colobus monkeys

COLOBUS MONKEY The word *colobus* comes from the Greek, meaning 'deformed', referring to the fact that this monkey lacks thumbs, grasping branches with just its four forward-facing fingers. This is impossible to discern from below, unlike its beautiful long, shaggy black-and-white coat and tail, for which it was much persecuted in days gone by.

Colobus troops live in forests with contiguous canopy, individuals making prodigious leaps from one tree to another. As with many animals, these troops normally comprise a dominant male, some females and their young. Anyone awake in the morning may hear them warming up with far-carrying calls resembling the winding of a clock!

SYKES' MONKEY There is no doubting that these monkeys' preferred habitat is highland forest, and so the best chance of finding them will be in the upland areas of Ngorongoro. They may also be encountered in riverine forest along the Mara River. Generally shiny blue-black in colour, sometimes with a pale neck collar, they live in large family troops of females and young, overseen by a single, much heavier male. When young males are ejected from their natal group, it seems they do not form bachelor troops, rather roaming around on their own until old enough to try and displace an established male from his harem.

Sykes' monkey

VERVET MONKEY There is no mistaking a male vervet monkey, although it will be harder to spot his red penis than his turquoise blue scrotum! Otherwise, all adult members of the species are distinguished by black faces, edged above with white.

Vervets are primarily arboreal but also quite at home on the ground, surviving on a mostly vegetarian diet, together with the occasional eggs, or even chicks, from any birds' nests they find.

The monkeys live communally, in large troops, comprising far fewer males than females. These are very hierarchical societies, which the young males tend to leave at about three years of age.

Mothers may have one young a year, occasionally twins, after a gestation period of around 165 days. Infants start life clinging to their mother's belly. Fellow troop members are all keen to hold and groom the young one, whom the mother is often happy to share around.

Vervets have a wide variety of calls signalling different dangers, particularly their principal predators – leopards, eagles, pythons and baboons. Mothers also recognise the scream of their own offspring.

 Lesser galago
 Greater galago

GALAGO Known as galagos or bushbabies, the members of the Galagidae family are all nocturnal primates, living arboreal lives. Huge, staring eyes and big, bat-like ears equip them for feeding at night, with diet depending to some extent on species. Greater galagos are mainly fruit and insect eaters and can be lured down to human-made feeding stations. Lesser galagos are particularly attracted to the resin secreted by injured trees, but will also eat fruits and insects.

They only inhabit areas where there are enough trees to enable them to travel around the territory without coming to the ground unless this is really necessary. They are very vulnerable to predation as it is, especially from owls and snakes and even other primates. Long tails, longer than head and body combined, help them balance as they bound or leap through the trees.

Being nocturnal, they are particularly dependent on species-specific vocal communication, and also mark their arboreal paths with urine.

Rock and bush hyraxes are found in rocky areas, whereas the tree hyrax prefers arboreal habitats.

HYRAX Famously the elephant's closest terrestrial relative, these are small, furry animals with no visible tail. More like guinea pigs, they are usually divided into rock, tree and bush hyraxes, and all species may be found in the region. The tree hyrax is mainly nocturnal, marking its territory with a piercing variety of screeches. Bush and rock hyraxes are diurnal and both species may occupy rocky outcrops, where the animals can warm themselves. Both species are prime prey for Verreaux's eagles.

MAMMALS

HARES Hares are distinguished from rabbits by being solitary animals that do not build burrows, preferring to lie up in long grass in the daytime and to hide from danger rather than run from it. They have long ears, and may show a white undertail. As these mammals are mainly nocturnal, the best chance of seeing one is in the headlights of the vehicle when returning late from a game drive.

SPRINGHARE These rodents are unmistakeable, resembling miniature kangaroos as they bound around on long back legs. They use their diminutive front ones, armed with five very sharp claws (four on the back legs), for digging. They are nocturnal, vegetarian and live in sandy soil burrows, which they usually excavate themselves.

Straw-coloured fruit bat

Wahlberg's epauletted fruit bat | Egyptian slit-faced bat

BATS Bats are flying mammals whose forelimbs are adapted as wings. They are essentially divided into those that echolocate (sometimes called microbats), using ultrasound to detect prey and navigate their surrounds, and those that don't (megabats or fruit bats). These bigger bats have well-developed eyesight to help them find fruit or nectar, and they play an important role as pollinators of, for example, sausage trees.

Most bats are nocturnal, roosting by day in caves or under eaves, but groups of larger megabats are sometimes visible in the daytime, hanging in trees, upside down by their feet.

Large ears enable bats to locate prey sounds, like fluttering moths' wings. Where there are many bats emerging from a roost, keep an eye out for a bat hawk!

Zebra mouse

Multimammate mouse

Gerbil

Four-striped grass mouse

SMALL MAMMALS Rodents are everywhere, but seeing them is a question of luck rather than skill. Confiding little zebra mice might be spotted scuttling from cover to cover, but gerbils, with their long hind legs, are more nocturnal. For some species, 'mouse' and 'rat' seem interchangeable, and sticking to the Latin name can avoid confusion. However, at least the English name of multimammate mouse or rat informs that the species

Grey climbing mouse

Pouched mouse

Black-and-rufous sengi

Short-snouted sengi

has many mammary glands, which its scientific name *Mastomys natalensis* does not! And, the pouch of a pouched mouse, or rat, is in its cheeks. Not only elephants, but also elephant shrews call Serengeti and Ngorongoro home. These will be hard to see, but there are certainly more of them than there are elephants. They are mouse-like rodents, also known as sengis, and characterised by long snouts.

A lone marabou stork watches the oncoming storm. This stork is just one of more than 500 bird species recorded in Serengeti and Ngorongoro. A wide variety of habitats at very different altitudes make this region a birdwatcher's paradise.

Martial eagle

EAGLES The martial eagle is a huge bird, often perching on treetops. If seen face on, distinctive black spots or streaks below a black breast easily separate it from the far smaller black-chested snake-eagle. The martial eagle also has feathered legs, with talons powerful enough to kill monkeys, small antelope and large ground birds. It will not hesitate to attack monitor lizards, venomous snakes and even jackals.

The bateleur answers every birdwatcher's prayer for a large, instantly recognisable raptor. Observing only one of its three most distinctive features – colour, shape or flight – is enough to confirm identification. Adults of both sexes have bright red feet and beaks, although their iconic black, white and chestnut plumage differs, especially the underwings. The name bateleur derives from the French word for juggler, and by extension, tightrope walker, alluding to the bird's seesawing flight pattern. This rocking motion compensates for the bird's lack of tail.

Perched Verreaux's eagles look all black, but white primary wing patches are evident when they glide along a cliff edge in search of their main prey, rock hyraxes.

Bateleur

Verreaux's eagle

Brown snake-eagle

Black-chested snake-eagle

Black-chested snake-eagle

SNAKE-EAGLES A fairly large raptor, perched upright and alone on top of a tall tree, might well be a snake-eagle. Both species pictured above are uncommon but widespread in Serengeti and Ngorongoro, where the western banded snake-eagle also occurs. When perched, the brown snake-eagle is indeed all brown, but in flight it shows silvery white underwings. A mature black-chested snake-eagle is easily identified – check that it has no spots on its belly. Bare legs separate it from the martial eagle.

AFRICAN FISH-EAGLE Widely distributed throughout sub-Saharan Africa, the African fish-eagle prefers lakes to rivers. Perched on a branch above the water, it scans the surface to spot live piscine prey, which it then swoops down to take feet first. Failing that, floating dead fish will do. If still unsuccessful, this bird won't hesitate to rob other fish-eaters, such as herons, hamerkops or ospreys, of their prey, or to hunt other birds. It may even attack flamingos.

SECRETARYBIRD It is near impossible to ignore a secretarybird when passing by one, nor to wonder why it is called what it is. Are its grey-and-black plumage or quill-like crests reminders of formal secretaries of early years, or is 'secretary' a corruption of its scientific name, *Sagittarius serpentarius*?

The secretarybird is the only raptor in Africa that searches for its prey on foot, usually in grassland, trampling it to death before consuming it then and there. Such hunting behaviour has turned secretarybirds into opportunistic feeders, and just about any creature they come across is fair game. Observations suggest that males and females hunt in pairs, unless she is on nest duty and her mate has to bring back food.

WHITE-BACKED VULTURE Easily the most common vulture in Serengeti and Ngorongoro, this species can be distinguished from others by its plain brown body and black beak. It is most likely to be confused with Rüppell's vulture, but the latter has a distinctive horn-coloured beak. The eponymous white back is visible only when the bird is flying, and then only in adults from above, so it is not a reliable species indicator.

White-backed vultures nest and roost in trees, which usually enables them to be first on the scene of any kill – unlike the cliff-living Rüppell's vultures that may have to travel from further away.

In recent years, vulture numbers have drastically reduced because they feed on poisoned bait illegally set out for predators. Less often, vultures are deliberately poisoned by poachers who fear the birds drawing attention to their illegal activities.

Hooded vultures

Palm-nut vulture

Lappet-faced vulture

LAPPET-FACED AND HOODED VULTURES The massive size of the lappet-faced vulture's bill and bare pink head are good indicators of this species, which takes its name from the folds of skin hanging down the sides of its head. It is a relatively solitary bird, and there are seldom more than two or three individuals around any one kill. They often tear into an intact carcass and so open it up for smaller vultures. By vulture standards, hooded vultures are very small, with dark pink heads. They are as likely to be seen around village rubbish dumps as on the edge of a kill, waiting for the larger species to have their fill.

PALM-NUT VULTURE This bird prefers living around rivers and captures its own food. Besides a wide variety of animal prey, its diet often includes the husks or fruits of different palms.

Southern white-faced owl

African scops-owl

Pearl-spotted owlet

Marsh owl

OWLS It is hard to spot owls in the daytime without help from a guide who knows where they roost. The southern white-faced owl has very large ears and is not as common as the smaller, but similar-looking, African scops-owl. Pearl-spotted owlets are partially diurnal, and if a mob of smaller birds look excited around some vegetation, it may be because there is an owlet within.

OSTRICH There is no mistaking an ostrich. Of the two species, common and Somali, only the former is found in Serengeti and Ngorongoro. The males are identified by black feathers and pink skin on the neck and legs. Females are grey-brown, not least the better to remain concealed as they sit on their nests in the daytime, the males taking over at night. Chicks are similarly coloured, as they follow behind the female, often for many

months. She may or may not be their mother as the young from several broods often form crèches.

Male ostriches utilise their substantial wings to great effect: they frantically flap them during courtship, both to attract females and to threaten encroaching males.

Ostriches nest in open grassland, the male scraping out a hollow before the female lays her off-white eggs.

Kori bustards

BUSTARDS Being essentially ground-dwellers, bustards are coloured to blend in with their terrestrial background, particularly the females, which incubate the eggs.

The kori bustard is easily distinguished by size alone. It is the heaviest flying bird in the world, made all the more extraordinary for its ability to take off from a standing start.

At midday, look for bustards under trees, resting in the shade. In the morning and evening, the birds are out and about, searching for all sorts of ground food.

Black-bellied bustard

White-bellied bustards

The male kori bustard is much larger than the female. Mating is preceded by elaborate courtship dances, during which the male cocks his tail and inflates his neck, puffing out the feathers into a white ruff.

Double-banded courser

Spotted thick-knee

Crested francolin

Red-necked spurfowl

GROUND BIRDS These birds spend most of their lives on the ground, nesting there as well, although guineafowl roost in trees, as may spurfowl.

Coursers and thick-knees are mainly nocturnal birds. In the case of the thick-knee, this is easy to deduce from its particularly large eyes. Francolins and spurfowl are generally diurnal, living in family groups. They often prefer to run rather than fly away from danger. There are three species of spurfowl that might be seen in the region (red-necked, yellow-necked and grey-breasted), and two francolins (coqui and crested).

Crowned lapwings

Chestnut-bellied sandgrouse

Helmeted guineafowl

Helmeted guineafowl are unmistakeable, not least because they are very sociable, living in large groups.

The habits of sandgrouse are fascinating, particularly those of the males, which gather at waterholes in large flocks. They soak their breasts before flying back to give the young a drink from their feathers. As is often the case with ground birds, female sandgrouse are more muted in their coloration so that they can blend into the background while sitting on their nests.

With their crowns and red beaks, crowned plovers are more distinctive birds and compensate for this by being more aggressive.

GREY CROWNED CRANE These birds' haunting cries ring out often in early morning, as pairs fly out of their treetop roosts to spend the day feeding in damp grassland. They are devoted parents until the chicks fledge, having gradually acquired their golden crown and unmistakeable face. This is the national bird of Uganda and the only crane to be found regularly in East Africa.

SOUTHERN GROUND HORNBILL Only distantly related to other hornbills, ground hornbills live most of the day in small family groups on open grassland, foraging for food. They are omnivorous and will eat almost anything, from snails and termites to frogs and snakes, using their beak to break hard food items into smaller pieces. Before dawn, they often call out with a distinctive *boom, boom, boom boom*.

Both males and females have white primary wing feathers, difficult to see when strutting around, but clearly visible in flight. Females can be identified by a small blue throat patch, while juveniles have a yellow face and throat.

FLAMINGOS Of the six flamingo species in the world, only the lesser and greater flamingos are found in Africa. Depending on the availability of water sources, thousands of flamingos flock to the Serengeti plains and Ngorongoro Crater each year. The birds often breed in Lake Natron, which is not far away on the Kenya border, and from where they may sometimes be seen commuting in big V-formation flocks, their necks outstretched.

Since the two species feed on different food items, they mix freely where they occur together. The lesser flamingo survives on a diet of blue-green algae, filtered from the upper surface of the water, whereas the greater flamingo feeds at deeper levels on slightly larger morsels, such as insect larvae and brine shrimps. The diet of the lesser flamingo is responsible for the rich pink colouring.

If the two species are seen together, the contrast in size is particularly pronounced. The adult lesser flamingo's dark bill is also very different from the greater's bicoloured one.

Greater flamingo

Lesser flamingo

MARABOU STORK This bird is impossible to confuse with any other, and is particularly recognisable by its enormous grey-brown beak and bare pink skin on the head and neck, down which hangs an inflatable air sac. The bare skin enables the marabou to bury its head in carcasses or urban landfills without soiling any feathers, in the same way as vultures do.

Occasionally single birds turn up, but generally marabous live and feed in large groups and nest colonially in tall acacia trees, both in the wild and in urban areas. In Serengeti and Ngorongoro, they may gather around rivers where wildebeest cross, in expectation of easy pickings. They also hang around the edge of kills, hoping to pick up pieces when other carnivores have gone.

Marabous are easily recognised in flight: unlike other storks, which fly with their necks outstretched, marabous fly with theirs retracted, like herons and egrets. Look for these huge storks on wetland edges, river banks and even on garbage dumps.

Yellow-billed stork

STORKS The yellow-billed stork is generally white, with a long yellow beak and bare red skin around its eyes. It is common in a wide variety of watery habitats, often seen standing motionless, with its beak open, as if awaiting prey to swim into it. Walking slowly through the water, it seems to feed by touch rather than sight, churning up the mud to disturb prey.

Of all the storks, it would be hard to imagine a more exotic-looking one than the saddle-billed stork. It is much less common than the yellow-billed.

Saddle-billed stork

Giant kingfisher

Pied kingfisher

KINGFISHERS AND HERONS Unlike several other kingfishers, the giant and pied feed exclusively in the water. The giant is the largest kingfisher in the world and fishes from a perch, unlike the pied, which is the only African kingfisher to hover over open water, so much increasing its chances of finding food.

Herons are familiar birds that, together with bitterns and egrets, make up the family Ardeidae – of which there are over 70 members. The goliath heron lives up to its name being the largest heron in the world, using its long, pointed beak to grab all sorts of aquatic prey.

Goliath heron

Blacksmith lapwings

African sacred ibis

Egyptian geese

African jacana

Purple swamphen

Great white pelicans

Red-billed teal

Little grebe

IN, ON AND AROUND THE WATER Birds exploit aquatic habitats in different ways. Some, like the African sacred ibis or blacksmith lapwing, peck around the water's edge, hardly getting their feet wet; jacanas seem almost to walk on the surface with their long toes, and swamphens are true paddlers. Pelicans fish from the surface, little grebes dive for food, the red-billed teal dabbles in the shallows, and the Egyptian goose is as at home with its family on the surface as when grazing on dry land.

Red-billed firefinch

Common waxbill

Speckled mousebird

Red-and-yellow barbet

Little bee-eater

Kenya rufous sparrow

BUSH AND WOODLAND BIRDS The red-and-yellow barbet is among the most colourful birds of the East African bush, with a red beak, red head above a yellow body, and white cheek patches. Barbets often give themselves away by their noisy duets, sung from the top of bushes or termite mounds.

Mousebirds are unmistakeable and abundant. Groups play follow-the-leader from bush to bush, and few birds look to be enjoying life more than these!

Red-billed firefinches are found in a variety of habitats, while waxbills are more at home in long grass. Rufous sparrows are ground-feeders and common in well-vegetated areas.

The bee-eaters are a fascinating family. As their name suggests, they catch insects in flight. Several species are northern migrants, so are only found in the region between October and April. The little bee-eaters are resident, and nearly always found in pairs. They perch on top of bushes, swooping down to catch prey and hunting much closer to the ground than other bee-eater species.

Above: Red-billed hornbill

Below: Von der Decken's hornbill

Green woodhoopoe

African hoopoe

HORNBILLS Very little of wild Africa does not host a hornbill of one species or another and, with their thick, differently coloured beaks (red, yellow or black) and varying wing patterns (plain or spotted), these are usually not hard to identify. Von der Decken's hornbill is distinguished from all others by a pale tip to the male's red beak (the female's is all black) and no spots on its wings. This species is most often seen in open woodland, where individuals or family parties move from one tree canopy to another.

Nearly all hornbills nest in tree cavities, into which, after mating, the female seals herself, the male bringing her food as she incubates the eggs.

WOODHOOPOE AND HOOPOE Green woodhoopoes live in noisy family parties, following one another from tree to tree, cackling as they go. Hoopoes, which take their name from the male's breeding-season call, are usually solitary birds, seen pecking away on the ground or flying off to a tree-hole nest. With their exotic crest, deep chestnut plumage and black-and-white wings, they are quite unmistakeable.

VILLAGE WEAVER Several black-faced or black-headed weavers fill the pages of field guides. To distinguish one species from another, check out in particular the extent of the black over the head (whole head, hood, head and throat) and eye colour (red or yellow). Village weavers have a black hood, tapering down the throat, and red eyes. They are also colonial, noisy nesters, often found close to human habitation, where they may gain protection from predators. They nest over water as well. Village weaver nests often incorporate a distinctive entrance tube.

Red-billed queleas

Lesser masked weaver

Red-headed weaver

WEAVERS AND QUELEAS Other than the red-headed weaver, weavers are almost all predominantly yellow. Species are often best identified by the males in breeding plumage. Queleas are smaller than weavers and often seen in huge flocks. The red-billed queleas pictured above are all breeding males.

All weaver nests are species-specific, both as to shape and materials. The red-headed weaver uses coarse twigs, and often finishes with a very long entrance tube, while the lesser masked weaver makes an untidy nest with a much shorter entrance.

Common bulbul

Yellow-billed oxpeckers

Common fiscal

BULBULS, OXPECKERS AND SHRIKES Common bulbuls are indeed found almost everywhere in East Africa, and often sing or show themselves when most other birds are resting and silent.

Several species of shrike occur in the region, all carnivorous. The common fiscal is a solitary, bush-top-perching bird, its plain black-and-white plumage separating it from other shrikes, which usually include some grey or brown in their feathers.

Red-billed or yellow-billed oxpeckers scrabble around on the backs of large herbivores searching for insects.

Superb starlings

Variable sunbird

Beautiful sunbird

STARLINGS AND SUNBIRDS The region's most abundant starling, superb starlings are widespread in a variety of bushed habitats.

Sunbirds are lively, always on the move in search of nectar or insects. Variable sunbirds are common at higher altitudes. The beautiful sunbird is more likely found lower down, the male's shiny green plumage highlighted by a bright red chest with golden patches on either side. A long tail completes the picture, which is a feature that even the yellow-breasted, non-breeding males retain.

The Serengeti crocodiles (*mamba* in Swahili), particularly those in the Mara and Grumeti rivers, are treated to twice-yearly feasts during the wildebeest and zebra migrations, so it is no surprise that they are some of the biggest in Africa.

NILE CROCODILE This large reptile is a fearsome hunter, seizing and drowning wildebeest and zebra as they attempt river crossings during migrations. It also feeds on animals that are trampled during these crossings. When not indulged by migrations, Nile crocodiles may have to hunt by stealth. They wait, submerged, by favoured bankside drinking spots, to grab an animal – even a human – coming down to the water. They feed on fish too. Crocodiles are very good swimmers, able to remain underwater for up to 45 minutes.

A female lays 30–50 hard-shelled eggs, upon which she keeps a watchful eye. The incubation period ranges from 80 to 100 days, depending on temperature, which, fascinatingly, also determines the sex of the young. On hatching, the mother takes her young to the water by carrying them in her mouth, so protecting them in the dangerous journey from the nest.

NILE MONITOR This is the longest lizard in Africa, sometimes exceeding 2m. While varied in colour, all monitors develop clear pale stripes, particularly on the tail. A forked tongue flicks out of powerful jaws that, along with the sharp claws, are ideally designed for hunting or defence. Nile monitors feed on fish, frogs, small reptiles and even crocodile eggs. If after the latter, monitors usually work in pairs. One distracts the mother crocodile, while the other digs out her eggs. When it comes to producing their own eggs, females may lay up to 60, often in an occupied termite mound, where the eggs are kept warm before hatching seven or eight months later.

FLAP-NECKED CHAMELEON

This species has no horns and is named for the ear flaps down the sides of its face. It is generally green in colour and is large as chameleons go, with an average length of around 25cm. It lives in bushes and trees but is often seen crossing roads. Like most chameleons, it lives predominantly on a diet of insects. In turn, it might make a meal for a boomslang.

The flap-necked chameleon is a species much in demand in the international pet trade.

Rock agama

Tree agama

AGAMAS These are medium-sized lizards, represented by some 40 species in mainly sub-Saharan Africa. The rock agamas are best searched for on flat rock slabs or kopjes, where the pink-headed, blue-bodied males may be sunning themselves or displaying to one or more drably coloured females. Male agamas' colouring tends to become much more vivid when mating. Tree agamas have adapted well to life around human habitation, as have the rock agamas.

Black-necked spitting cobra

Spotted bush snake

Mozambique spitting cobra

SNAKES Snakes are long and limbless reptiles, often loosely grouped as either venomous or non-venomous. The latter species may still give a nasty bite, but not a life-threatening one.

Snakes may be front-fanged or back-fanged. Those with fangs at the back of their mouths are typically not dangerous, not least because it takes a huge bite to get the back fangs to puncture skin. The boomslang, meaning 'tree snake', derived from the Afrikaans name for this species in South Africa, is a prominent exception, being both back-fanged and highly venomous.

Black mamba

Boomslang

Herald snake

Most of the highly venomous snakes, such as cobras and vipers, are front-fanged, making it much easier to deliver their venom. The locally common black-necked spitting cobra not only bites, but is also able to shoot a spray of venom directly from its fangs.

East Africa is home to the longest venomous snake in Africa – the black mamba. It is not common in Serengeti and Ngorongoro, however, and is a shy creature. Despite its highly toxic venom and fearsome reputation, a mamba that encounters a human is more likely to wriggle away than to strike.

AFRICAN ROCK PYTHON The best chance of spotting this snake – the largest in Africa – is to find it slithering across the road in front of your vehicle. Otherwise, look for it basking on rocks in the sun, quite often near water. Rock pythons are coloured a mix of brown, beige and grey, but size alone identifies them. There are a lot of contenders for the longest, their claims unverified, but let's say a specimen measuring 6m is very long!

Rock pythons have no fangs, but with over 80 sharp teeth, they can give a nasty bite with jaws that can dislocate when swallowing particularly large prey. These snakes are ambush hunters, biting their prey before wrapping their body around it and squeezing the animal to death. Young pythons eat lizards, birds and frogs, but larger ones can tackle a full-grown gazelle, which may take weeks to travel all the way through the snake's digestive tract.

Marsh terrapin

TERRAPINS These are freshwater turtles, although the difference between the two is blurred and some sources use either word for the same creature. They are essentially aquatic, but come out to bask on logs or sandbanks, plopping straight back into the water when disturbed. They have legs rather than flippers, with large webbed feet, equipping them well for walking on land. Most terrapins are omnivorous, feeding on a variety of aquatic plants, insects, small fish and carrion. They have quite often been seen seizing birds coming down to drink.

LEOPARD TORTOISE With a much more domed shell than the terrapins, this tortoise is one of the largest in the world and probably the biggest in Africa. Its black and sandy brown shell may be spotted in the drier, more open parts of Serengeti, moving slowly from one grazing area to another. When threatened, it retracts its head and legs into the shell, making it almost impossible for any predator to get a hold. However, when it is time to mate, the male seems to have no difficulty in mounting the female in the normal manner, often squeaking loudly in the process.

Juvenile leopard tortoise

Adult leopard tortoise

Banded rubber frog

Natal puddle frog

Platanna

Guttural toad

Plimpton's dainty frog

FROGS Frogs belong to the order Anura, derived from Greek and meaning 'without tail'. There is surely no other order with such imaginatively named members. Guttural toads are all over East Africa, and who cannot want to know more about the foam-nest tree frog, snoring puddle frog or Plimpton's dainty frog? All toads are frogs, but not all frogs are toads. Toads are identified by thick, dry, warty skin, which retains moisture and so allows them to live in drier habitats, and it is not unusual to find them hopping around lit buildings at night. Frogs have longer legs, built for jumping, and much moister skin. Some frogs are often well camouflaged, while others, such as the banded rubber frog, are vividly coloured to advertise their toxicity and deter predators.

Right: Female foam-nest tree frogs produce a frothy nest into which the eggs are laid. After hatching, tadpoles drop into the water below.

Foam-nest tree frog

INSECTS

DUNG BEETLES There are literally thousands of species of dung beetle, all over the world, and one of those most likely to be encountered on safari is the sacred dung beetle, or sacred scarab. It creates balls of dung much bigger than itself. Male and female beetles work together to roll away and bury these balls, after which the female lays her eggs – usually one in each ball. Balls act as a food store for adults and newly hatched young.

In other dung beetle species, only the male does the rolling, while the female rides on her suitor's ball. Still other dung beetles bury dung where they find it or otherwise excavate tunnels underneath dung piles.

The size of a dung beetle depends on the species. Small ones might measure only 5mm, large ones six times that. Pushing many times their own weight, dung beetles are among the strongest insects in the world.

African queen

Brown-veined white

Eyed ringlet

Round-winged orange tip

BUTTERFLIES There are four distinct stages to a butterfly's life: egg, larva (caterpillar), chrysalis (pupa) and adult. After mating, the adult lays her eggs on a leaf or stem, sometimes that of a very specific plant. The eggs then hatch into small caterpillars, each shedding its skin four or five times as it enlarges.

Once grown, caterpillars create a chrysalis around themselves. This is a hard protective case from which the fully fledged flying butterfly finally emerges.

The lifespan of a small butterfly in the tropics is two to three weeks. Species that hibernate a full winter in colder climes live much longer.

African caper white

Broad-bordered grass yellow

Citrus swallowtail

Yellow pansy

One or more of the species of orange tip is likely to be seen visiting flowers after the rains, as might very similar scarlet and magenta tips. Yellow pansies and eyed ringlets are easy to identify, and citrus swallowtails might turn up in a variety of different habitats, and if they aren't around, one or more of their distinctive long-tailed relatives is likely to be.

Not only do the wildebeest migrate within Serengeti, but when conditions are right, snowstorms of brown-veined whites may also pass over the savannah. Africa has its own monarch butterfly too, known colloquially as the African queen and closely resembling its famous north American relative.

HORSE FLIES Any big, biting fly tends to be labelled a 'horse fly', including those more strictly described as 'clegs'. Only the female inflicts painful bites on large mammals (including humans). Horse fly bites are immediately apparent, unlike mosquito bites, which are often only felt when the biter has gone.

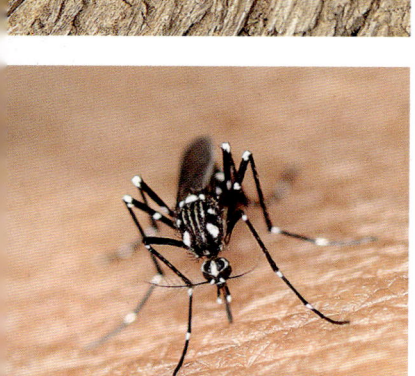

GRASS MOSQUITOES A damp, dark and cool environment may harbour these black mosquitoes, decorated with white spots on their joints and around their bodies. They bite freely in the daytime and evening but not at night, and are not vectors of malaria.

SMALL STINGLESS BEES These are smaller than conventional bees, and while lacking stings, they can bite. They also produce honey, much valued for its therapeutic benefits to such an extent that these tiny bees are being increasingly kept commercially. They feed on pollen and nectar, which they carry back to tree-cavity nests on their hind legs. These bees are colloquially known as 'sweat bees' for their taking salts from damp patches on the ground or around a human face!

SAFARI ANTS *Siafu* in Swahili, these have a justifiably fearsome reputation in East Africa for the painful bites of soldier ants. So powerful are the soldier's jaws that they are used in traditional societies as sutures: a person gets the ant to bite over a wound, then removes its body, leaving behind the ant's head with jaws pinching the skin together.

Safari ants travel in long columns, especially after the rains, with the blind soldiers guarding the smaller ants that are carrying food back to the colony. Male safari ants morph into bloated, flying 'sausage flies', departing the colony soon after hatching and often attracted by distant bright lights.

STICK INSECTS Occurring all over the warmer parts of the world, stick insects use shape as a camouflage, gently feeling their way along twigs and branches on six long legs, any one of which they can regenerate after an accident. They are very weak flyers. Females of many species can reproduce on their own, but unfertilised female eggs can only hatch into females. One or more of the species of stick insect should be present in Serengeti and its surrounds, but it takes a patient walk to find them.

 Common locust
 Paper wasp
 Cotton stainer

LOCUSTS Locusts are short-horned grasshoppers and some, like the milkweed locusts, are almost the size of small birds. Common garden locusts are also large, generally creamy brown, and can be quite startling with their noisy flight. From a look at close quarters, it will be apparent that their back legs are covered in prominent spines.

PAPER WASPS These long-bodied wasps take their name from their large papery nests, which are built from masticated plant material converted into many hexagonal cells. Each of these may contain a single larva, the whole nest tended by several females. Nests are built under the eaves of buildings or in other sheltered places, around which the wasps can be quite aggressive, inflicting painful stings.

COTTON STAINERS These are named from the nymphs' and adults' habit of feeding on seeds inside developing cotton bolls. There are many species around the world. One of the best known in Africa is distinctly marked in beige and black, and often found joined with another in copulation. Nymphs are bright red, with black markings, and feed in large clusters, with adults sometimes nearby.

RHINOCEROS BEETLES These beetles occur on every continent except Antarctica, and one of the most prominent species in East Africa is shiny red or brown in colour. It is often seen in palm trees along river banks. Its larvae are white grubs, which feed on decomposing vegetation.

Male rhinoceros beetles are larger than females, and it is hard to believe such beetles can fly, but they can, albeit clumsily. They may sometimes be found collapsed, wings beating frantically, near outside lights around camps and lodges. Only the males have horns, which they may use to intimidate rivals.

Larva

Plants provide food, shelter and shade for animals, but are fascinating in their own right too. Lone trees, such as this euphorbia on the edge of Ngorongoro Crater, attract immediate attention, as do plants in bloom. Otherwise, it will take a more inquisitive look at the vegetation around a kopje, in denser woodland or along a river bank to identify specific species.

SAUSAGE TREE Don't picnic under a fruiting sausage tree, because its huge seed pods can weigh anything up to 8kg and may plummet to the ground. The nasty-smelling maroon flowers are pollinated by fluttering bats at night. Unripe fruits are poisonous, but people split the ripe fruits into two and dry them out to make a traditional liquor. Sausage trees are found both along the edges of watercourses and out on open plains.

WHISTLING THORN This is generally a small, bushy species, producing large galls from which sizeable white spines protrude. Many of these galls are hollow, having been taken over by ants, whose entry and exit holes are said to produce a whistle when the wind blows. The ants benefit from a home, and in exchange may swarm out of the holes to attack feeding mammals, protecting the tree from excessive grazing by herbivores such as giraffes.

CANDELABRA EUPHORBIA These succulent trees grow up to 15m high and are widely distributed all the way down to South Africa. They have fleshy branches with four ridges on each, along which are small spines; these thorn-like structures may be absent on older, thicker trunks. Like other members of the Euphorbiaceae family, the branches produce a very poisonous white sap, which can cause blindness if it gets into human or animal eyes.

YELLOW FEVER TREE

These yellow-barked trees grow easily in swampy areas, where mosquitoes may breed, bringing the early explorers who passed by these trees to link them with their catching malaria. The trees were immortalised by English writer Rudyard Kipling in his description of a river in South Africa: 'the great grey-green, greasy Limpopo, all set about with fever trees'!

This species is known to attract an array of birds.

WILD DATE PALM Alternatively known as the Senegal date palm, these multitrunked trees grow in thick clumps along river or other wetland banks.

As with other palms, the leaves can be made into baskets and mats, and in parts of Africa the sap is harvested for palm wine. The edible orange fruits (dates) are around 2cm long and grow in dense hanging clusters. The thick foliage provides birds with cover and nest sites. This tree is often planted in gardens.

STRANGLER FIG More trees of the uplands, the name describes several different species in the genus *Ficus* which all start life when a seed excreted by a visiting bird germinates in the fork of a host tree. Initially, it is an epiphyte, extracting nourishment from the atmosphere rather than its host. Its aerial roots ultimately drop down to the ground and begin funnelling nutrition up to the fig. What was once a root starts to function as a trunk, slowly encasing its host and ultimately strangling it.

The fruit of strangler figs often grows straight out of the trunks or thicker branches, turning yellow or purple and becoming a big attraction for birds and monkeys.

Strangler figs are often important ceremonial trees to the communities living around them.

COMMIPHORA Also known as African myrrh, this is a knobbly, deciduous shrub or tree that seldom grows more than 5m tall. It has spine-tipped branches and papery bark that peels away to reveal a green layer underneath. The tree can photosynthesise through its trunk and branches. It grows in drier areas of savannah and is of particular importance to local people for the medicinal properties of its resin, bark and fruit. The leaves are high in unpalatable tannin and are not grazed by game animals.

ALOES In any dry part of Africa there is likely to be an aloe of one kind or another. *Aloe secundiflora* (left) is a solitary species, growing in rocky areas or well-drained soil. Its leaves are unspotted and tinted in varying shades of green with darker, and very sharp, spines on their edges. The pink flowers point upwards and grow on stems up to 2m high. *Aloe volkensii* (right) is much taller, with several stems growing from the same base and reaching a height of up to 9m. It has more orangey flowers.

UMBRELLA THORN These beautiful flat-topped thorntrees are symbolic of the African bush. They have both hooked and straight thorns, but are more easily identified by their distinctive curling, twisted seed pods, much favoured by both livestock and wild animals. The animals will take the pods from the trees if they can reach them, otherwise off the ground. Earlier the trees will have burst into a mass of white or pale yellow flowers – a magnet for many different birds and insects.

Glossary

Canid: Member of the family Canidae, which includes dogs, jackals and foxes

Carnivore: Animal that feeds on the flesh of other animals

Colonial: Living in groups or colonies

Crepuscular: Active at dawn and dusk

Cud: Food brought up from the first stomach of a ruminant for continued chewing

Diurnal: Active during the daytime (as opposed to nocturnal)

Epiphyte: A plant growing on another plant and gaining sustenance from air or water (contrast with parasite which derives nutrients from its host)

Gregarious: Living in groups or loosely organised communities

Herbivore: Animal that feeds on plants

Incisors: Teeth at the front of the jaw, used for cutting and tearing food

Insectivorous: Of animals and birds, feeding on insects and other invertebrates

Invertebrate: An animal without a backbone – such as worms, snails, insects and spiders

Matriarch: Older female animal (usually elephant) which is head of the family group

Musth: Relating to elephants – a condition in bulls characterised by aggressive sexual behaviour and associated with discharge from a gland between ear and eye

Natal herd: The social group into which an animal is born

Nocturnal: Active by night (as opposed to diurnal)

Omnivore: An animal that eats food of both plant and animal origin

Quadruped: Four-legged animal

Ruminant: Animal with more than one stomach, which swallows food and then brings it back up again to continue chewing (the cud)

Rut: The period of the year, also known as the mating season, when animals display an urge to breed and which often leads to males competing for sexual access to females

Terrestrial: Living on the ground

Thermoregulation: The ability to maintain a constant body temperature

Picture credits

AS = adobestock.com, DJM = Dino J. Martins, WC = via Wikimedia Commons
b = bottom, c = centre, l = left, r = right, t = top, m = middle

Title page: Nick Dale/AS
4: andreanita/AS
9: Radek/AS
12–13: Rixie/AS
16 t: adogslifephoto/AS
31 tr: Nick Dale/AS
38–39: olyasolodenko/AS
48 b: Ozkan Ozmen/AS
68: Danita Delimont/AS
78 b: Hu Chen on Unsplash
83: Danita Delimont/AS
86 b: Elena/AS
90: hugo/AS
91 both: Martin Mecnarowski/AS
92 t: Travel Stock/AS
94 tl: Karlos Lomsky/AS, **tc:** Tyrone/AS, **tr:** Nadine Haase/AS, **bl:** Nadine Wagner/AS, **br:** Sergio/SA
95 tl: alfotokunst/AS, **tc:** Guillaume/AS, **tr:** Impala/AS, **ml:** andreanita/AS, **bc:** Gunter/AS, **br:** henk bogaard/AS
103 t: Photocreo Bednarek, **b:** Nadine Wagner/AS
107: Santiago Vigo/AS
109 tl: EcoView/AS, **tr:** slowmotiongli/AS
111 bl: Bernard DUPONT from FRANCE, CC BY-SA 2.0/WC, **br:** EcoView/AS
112: David/AS
113 tr: bereta/AS
114 tl: Charles J. Sharp, CC BY-SA 4.0, WC, **tr:** nicoloperazzo/AS, **bl:** Mahomed Desai, CC BY 4.0/WC, **br:** InnerPeace/AS
115 tl: Telegro, CC BY-SA 4.0/WC, **tr:** Bernard DUPONT from FRANCE, CC BY-SA 2.0/WC, **bl:** phototrip.cz/AS, **br:** Andrew Keys, CC BY-SA 4.0/WC
119 l: James Heupel and Danita Delimont/AS, **r:** Nick Dale/AS
122: phototrip.cz/AS
123 t: naturespy/AS
124: Dmitrii Zhodzishskii on Unsplash
126: Chris Brignell/AS
127 tr: PACO COMO/AS, **bl:** Riaan van den Berg/AS
128–9: EastVillageImages/AS
130 bl: Lori Labrecque/AS
131: Guillaume/AS
132 bl: Andy Morffew from Itchen Abbas, Hampshire, UK, CC BY 2.0/WC
133 tl: Reabetswe Matjeke/Wirestock/AS
139 l: Klaus Heidemann/Wirestock/AS
140 b: nyiragongo/AS
141: Ludwig/AS
142 tr: David/AS, **br:** Peter/AS
143 bl: Alta Oosthuizen/AS
144 tl: PIOTR/AS, **m:** Thomas/AS
145 r: Francesco Veronesi from Italy, CC BY-SA 2.0/WC
147 l: mauro53/AS
148: slowmotiongli/AS
149 bl: PIOTR/AS, **br:** henk bogaard/AS
150 tr: Nick Dale/AS
151 t: Danita Delimont/AS, **br:** Nigel Voaden from UK, CC BY SA 2.0/WC
152–3: justasc/AS
154 t: Maciej Sobczak/AS, **b:** pifate/AS
155 t: gudkovandrey/AS
158 b: Mathias/AS
159 l: Nadine Wagner/AS
160 t: Nick Dale/AS, **bl:** Bernard DUPONT from FRANCE, CC BY-SA 2.0/WC, **br:** Craig/AS
161 t and br: Craig/AS, **bl:** stuporter/AS
162 t: FotoRequest/AS, **b:** poco_bw/AS
165 t: Janos/AS, **b:** Jeffrey Banke/AS
166 tl, tr, b: Alan Channing, **ml:** Craig/AS, **mr:** Marius Burger/WC
167 t: Bernard DUPONT from FRANCE, CC BY-SA 2.0/WC **b:** Alan Channing
169: bennymarty/AS
170–175 all: DJM
178 ml: Kobus/AS
179: Kaitlind/AS
180 both: Anne Powys
181: Anne Powys
183 mr and br: SAplants, CC BY-SA 4.0/WC
184 l: James/AS, **r:** DJM
185 both: DJM
186: Quentin Luke
187 l: Nigel Pavitt, **r:** Anne Powys
Back cover bl: danmir12/AS

References

Kennedy, A.S. & Kennedy V. 2014. *Animals of the Serengeti and Ngorongoro Conservation Area*. New Jersey: Princeton University Press.

Kennedy, A.S. 2014. *Birds of the Serengeti and Ngorongoro Conservation Area*. New Jersey: Princeton University Press.

Kingdon, J. 2016. *The Kingdon Pocket Guide to African Mammals*. London: Bloomsbury Wildlife.

Martins, D. 2014. *Insects of East Africa*. South Africa: Struik Nature

Scott, J. & A. 2012. *Safari Guide to East African Animals*. Nairobi: Kensta.

Spawls, S., Howell, K. Drewes, R. & Ashe, J. 2002. *A Field Guide to the Reptiles of East Africa*. London: Academic Press.

Stevenson, T. & Fanshawe J. 2020. *Birds of East Africa: Kenya, Tanzania, Uganda, Rwanda, Burundi*. Helm Field Guides. London: Bloomsbury Publishing.

Index

BIRDS
- Barbet, red-and-yellow 144
- Bateleur 119
- Bee-eater, little 145
- Bulbul, common 150
- Bustard, black-bellied 130
- Bustard, kori 130
- Bustard, white-bellied 130
- Courser, double-banded 132
- Crane, grey crowned 134
- Eagle, martial 118
- Eagle, Verreaux's 119
- Firefinch, red-billed 144
- Fiscal, common 150
- Fish-eagle, African 121
- Flamingo, greater 137
- Flamingo, lesser 137
- Francolin, crested 132
- Goose, Egyptian 142
- Grebe, little 143
- Guineafowl, helmeted 133
- Heron, goliath 140
- Hoopoe, African 147
- Hornbill, red-billed 146
- Hornbill, southern ground 135
- Hornbill, Von der Decken's 146
- Ibis, African sacred 142
- Jacana, African 142
- Kingfisher, giant 140
- Kingfisher, pied 140
- Lapwing, blacksmith 142
- Lapwing, crowned 133
- Mousebird, speckled 144
- Ostrich 128
- Owl, marsh 127
- Owl, southern white-faced 126
- Owlet, pearl-spotted 127
- Oxpecker, yellow-billed 150
- Pelican, great white 143
- Quelea, red-billed 149
- Sandgrouse, chestnut-bellied 133
- Scops-owl, African 127
- Secretarybird 122
- Snake-eagle, black-chested 120
- Snake-eagle, brown 120
- Sparrow, Kenya rufous 145
- Spurfowl, red-necked 132
- Starling, superb 151
- Stork, marabou 138
- Stork, saddle-billed 139
- Stork, yellow-billed 139
- Sunbird, beautiful 151
- Sunbird, variable 151
- Swamphen, purple 142
- Teal, red-billed 143
- Thick-knee, spotted 132
- Vulture, hooded 125
- Vulture, lappet-faced 125
- Vulture, palm-nut 125
- Vulture, white-backed 124
- Waxbill, common 144
- Weaver, lesser masked 149
- Weaver, red-headed 149
- Weaver, village 148
- Woodhoopoe, green 147

FROGS
- Dainty frog, Plimpton's 166
- Platanna 166
- Puddle frog, Natal 166
- Rubber frog, banded 166
- Toad, guttural 166
- Tree frog, foam-nest 167

INSECTS
- Ant, safari 173
- Bee, small stingless 172
- Beetle, dung 168
- Beetle, rhinoceros 175
- Butterfly, African caper white 171
- Butterfly, African queen 170
- Butterfly, broad-bordered grass yellow 171
- Butterfly, brown-veined white 170

Butterfly, citrus swallowtail 171
Butterfly, eyed ringlet 170
Butterfly, round-winged orange tip 170
Butterfly, yellow pansy 171
Cotton stainer 174
Fly, horse 172
Locust, common 174
Mosquito, grass 172
Stick insect 173
Wasp, paper 174

MAMMALS
Aardwolf 83
Antelope 94
Baboon, olive 104
Bat, Egyptian slit-faced 113
Bat, straw-coloured fruit 112
Bat, Wahlberg's epauletted fruit 113
Buffalo, African 50
Caracal 79
Cheetah 66
Civet 91
Dik-dik, Naivasha 94
Duiker, grey 95
Eland 94, 100
Elephant 26
Fox, bat-eared 84
Galago, greater 109
Galago, lesser 109
Gazelle, Grant's 95, 99
Gazelle, Thomson's 95, 98
Genet, small-spotted 90
Gerbil 114
Giraffe 42
Hare 111
Hartebeest, Coke's 94, 102
Hippopotamus 38
Honey badger 89
Hyaena, spotted 80
Hyaena, striped 82
Hyrax 110
Impala 95
Jackal, black-backed 87
Jackal, golden 88
Jackal, side-striped 86
Klipspringer 94, 103
Leopard 72
Lion 54
Mongoose, banded 92
Mongoose, dwarf 92
Mongoose, slender 92
Monkey, colobus 106
Monkey, Sykes' 107
Monkey, vervet 108
Mouse, four-striped grass 114
Mouse, grey climbing 115
Mouse, multimammate 114
Mouse, pouched 115
Mouse, zebra 114
Nyala 94
Oribi 95
Reedbuck, bohor 95
Rhinoceros, black 36
Sengi, black-and-rufous 115
Sengi, short-snouted 115
Serval 79
Springhare 111
Steenbok 94
Topi 95
Warthog 48
Waterbuck, defassa 95
Wild cat, African 79
Wildebeest, white-bearded 12
Zebra 20

PLANTS
Aloe secundiflora 187
Aloe volkensii 187
Commiphora 186
Euphorbia 176
Euphorbia, candelabra 181
Sausage tree 178
Strangler fig 185
Umbrella thorn 188
Whistling thorn 180
Wild date palm 184
Yellow fever tree 182

REPTILES
Agama, rock 159
Agama, tree 159
Boomslang 160
Bush snake, spotted 160
Chameleon, flap-necked 158
Cobra, black-necked spitting 160
Cobra, Mozambique spitting 160
Crocodile, Nile 154
Herald snake 161
Mamba, black 161
Monitor, Nile 156
Rock python, African 162
Terrapin, marsh 164
Tortoise, leopard 164